A
Literature Unit
for

Farmer
Boy

by Laura Ingalls Wilder

Written by Laurie Swinwood

Illustrated by Theresa M. Wright

Teacher Created Materials

P.O. Box 1040

Huntington Beach, CA 92647

© *1993 Teacher Created Materials, Inc.*

Made in U.S.A.

ISBN 1-55734-428-0

D1560885

Table of Contents

Introduction

A good book can touch our lives like a good friend. Within its pages are words and characters that can inspire us to achieve our highest ideals. We can turn to it for companionship, recreation, comfort, and guidance. It can also give us a cherished story to hold in our hearts forever.

In *Literature Units*, great care has been taken to select books that are sure to become good friends!

Teachers who use this literature unit will find the following features to supplement their own valuable ideas.

- Sample Lesson Plans

- Pre-reading Activities

- Biographical Sketch and Picture of the Author

- Book Summary

- Vocabulary Lists and Suggested Vocabulary Ideas

- Chapters grouped for study with each section including a (an):

  — *quiz*

  — *hands-on project*

  — *cooperative learning activity*

  — *cross-curricular connection*

  — *extension into the reader's life*

- Post-reading Activities

- Book Report Ideas

- Research Ideas

- Culminating Activities

- Three Different Options for Unit Tests

- Bibliography

- Answer Key

We are confident this unit will be a valuable addition to your planning, and we hope that as you use our ideas, your students will increase the circle of "friends" they have in books!

Sample Lesson Plan

Each of the lessons suggested below can take from one to several days to complete.

Lesson 1

- Introduce and complete some or all of the pre-reading activities found on page 5.
- Read "About the Author" with your students. (page 6)
- Introduce the vocabulary list for Section 1. (page 8)

Lesson 2

- Choose a Vocabulary Activity. (page 9)
- Read chapters 1-6. As you read, place the vocabulary words in the context of the story and discuss their meanings.
- Make fried apples 'n' onions. (page 11)
- Simulate a one-room schoolhouse. (page 12)
- Experiment with popcorn. (page 13)
- Take an imaginary trip. (page 14)
- Administer the quiz for Section 1. (page 10)
- Introduce the vocabulary list for Section 2. (page 8)

Lesson 3

- Read chapters 7-12. Place the vocabulary words in context and discuss their meanings.
- Create dioramas. (page 16)
- Choose a Vocabulary Activity. (page 9)
- Create life-sized characters. (page 17)
- Begin research projects. (page 18)
- Try an Almanzo simulation. (page 19)
- Administer the Section 2 quiz. (page 15)
- Introduce the vocabulary list for Section 3. (page 8)

Lesson 4

- Read chapters 13-18. Place the vocabulary words in context and discuss their meanings.
- Choose a Vocabulary Activity. (page 9)
- Make blueberry pudding. (page 21)
- Perform Readers' Theater. (page 22)
- Plant pumpkins. (page 23)
- Celebrate Independence Day. (page 24)
- Administer the Section 3 quiz. (page 20)
- Introduce the vocabulary list for Section 4. (page 8)

Lesson 5

- Read chapters 19-24. Place the vocabulary words in context and discuss their meanings.
- Choose a Vocabulary activity. (page 9)
- Make candles. (page 26)
- Create a model farm. (page 27)
- Create a poetry book. (page 28)
- Discover there's no place like home. (page 29)
- Administer the Section 4 quiz. (page 25)
- Introduce the vocabulary list for Section 5. (page 8)

Lesson 6

- Read chapters 25-29. Place the vocabulary words in context and discuss their meanings.
- Choose a Vocabulary activity. (page 9)
- Make a Farmer Boy doll. (page 31)
- Create a class quilt. (page 34)
- Take a field trip. (page 35)
- Complete the decision-making activity. (page 36)
- Administer the Section 5 quiz. (page 30)

Lesson 7

- Have a read-a-thon. (page 40)
- Discuss any questions your students may have about the story. (page 37)
- Assign book report and research projects. (pages 38-39)
- Begin work on the culminating activities. (pages 41-42)

Lesson 8

- Administer unit tests 1, 2, and/or 3. (pages 43-45)
- Discuss the test answers and responses.
- Discuss the students' opinions and enjoyment of the book.
- Provide a list of related reading for the students. (page 46)

Lesson 9

- Have a Wilder Celebration. (pages 41-42)

Before the Book

Children gain the most from any piece of literature when they are given a solid background before reading. They need to have a feel for the time period, the characters, and the author of the book. The following activities may work well with your class.

1. Create a Wilder bulletin board. Copy and enlarge the cover of *Farmer Boy* and place it in the center of the board. Place Wilder family photos around it. Write to the Almanzo and Laura Ingalls Wilder Association to find out about ordering photos of the Wilders.

    The Almanzo and Laura Ingalls Wilder Association
    P.O. Box 283,
    Malone, New York 12953.

2. Read *Little House in the Big Woods* to your class.

3. Discuss the term *pioneer* with your class. Share the importance of the westward movement and its impact on our country today.

4. The teacher can dress up as Laura Ingalls Wilder or Almanzo Wilder and have the children conduct an interview about Laura Ingalls Wilder. Have each student write a brief biography on Laura, based on the facts gained from the interview. For interview information see About the Author, page 6.

5. Visit an area farm.

6. Borrow pioneer trunks from your local museum and share authentic artifacts from the pioneer era with your students.

7. Predict what the story may be about by reading the title and studying the cover.

8. Discuss other books by Laura Ingalls Wilder that the students might have read.

9. Discuss the copyright, illustrator, and publisher.

10. Have your students write a letter to you, telling what they hope to learn from *Farmer Boy* and whether they think they will enjoy the book. Save the letters and share them with the students when you have finished reading the book.

About the Author

Laura Elizabeth Ingalls was born in a log cabin, in the "Big Woods" of Pepin, Wisconsin, on February 7, 1867. She was the second child born to Charles and Caroline Ingalls.

Pa Ingalls was restless. The pioneer spirit was strong within him. In the spring of 1870, he moved his family by covered wagon to Montgomery County, Kansas, "Indian Territory." They later moved back to Pepin; on to Plum Creek, (near Walnut Grove) Minnesota; to Burr Oak, Iowa; and back to Walnut Grove, Minnesota. In 1879, they settled in De Smet, South Dakota.

Laura started teaching school in 1883, when she was 15. She taught in an abandoned claim shanty, twelve miles from De Smet. At the age of 18, she married Almanzo Wilder, who was 28. They had a daughter, Rose, and a son, who died in infancy. In 1894, they settled at Rocky Ridge Farm in Mansfield, Missouri.

Laura became well recognized for her success in raising poultry. She became household editor for the "Missouri Ruralist." Her first article appeared in February, 1911; Laura had just turned 44. Her daughter, Rose, was a successful journalist. She encouraged Laura to write her autobiography.

Laura agreed to write about her childhood. On lined tablets, with a soft lead pencil, she wrote her story. It began in the Big Woods and ended on her wedding day in 1885. She called her story "Pioneer Girl." It was not accepted for publication. Laura decided to write a book for children about her own experiences as a pioneer child. She called it *Little House in the Big Woods*. Harper and Brother published the book in 1932. Laura was sixty-five years old. She was amazed by its success.

Children wrote to Laura begging her to write more. She decided to write of her husband's childhood, in Malone, New York. She called it *Farmer Boy*, and it was published in 1933. In 1935, she published *Little House on the Prairie*; in 1937, *On the Banks of Plum Creek*; in 1939, *By the Shores of Silver Lake*; in 1940, *The Long Winter*; and in 1941, *Little Town on the Prairie*; and *These Happy Golden Years*, in 1943.

Laura lived three days past her 90th birthday. She died on February 10, 1957. Though Laura's memories of the past provide us with many insights into pioneer life, she also had a keen vision of the future.

She wrote:

> *Many things have changed since I beat eggs with a fork or cleaned a kerosene lamp. But the truths we learned from our parents and the principles they taught us are always true; they can never change. Great improvements in living have been made because every American has been able to pursue his happiness, and so long as Americans are free they will continue to make our country ever more wonderful.*

Taken from the book, *Laura Ingalls Wilder* by William Anderson. (The Kipling Press, 1987)

Farmer Boy

by Laura Ingalls Wilder

(Harper & Row, 1933)

In the winter of 1866, in upstate New York, eight-year-old Almanzo, his brother Royal, and his sisters, Alice and Eliza Jane, make their way through the snow to a one-room schoolhouse located on Hardscrabble Hill. Their teacher is Mr. Corse whom Almanzo likes because he is gentle and doesn't whip children for not knowing their lessons. But Almanzo fears for Mr. Corse because a group of young hooligans, led by Big Bill Ritchie, like to cause trouble for the teacher each year. Mr. Corse's predecessor was beaten so badly that he died. Almanzo is afraid that the same will happen to Mr. Corse, but to Almanzo's surprise, with the help of Father's black-snake whip, Mr. Corse gives Big Bill Ritchie a licking he'll never forget.

Now, Almanzo enjoys going to school, but he would rather stay home. His father allows him to do so when there are various chores to be done around the farm. And so when Almanzo stays home, he works from sun up to sun down planting and cultivating, scrubbing floors, and breaking his young oxen, Star and Bright. Almanzo spends much time with the calves and teaches them not only to obey his commands, but to pull a loaded sled as well. This is all well and good, but Almanzo would really like to break a colt. He doesn't understand why, if he does such a fine job with Star and Bright, Father won't even let him near the colts. Nevertheless, Almanzo is determined to play with the colts and nearly gets his hide tanned in so doing.

Aside from all his chores, Almanzo still finds time to enjoy himself swimming, picking berries, and sledding in the winter time. The life that Almanzo leads is a serene one, and he wouldn't trade it for anything. It is certain that Almanzo knows an abundance about farming—everything from churning butter and planting potatoes, to raising oxen and harvesting maple sugar. So when Mr. Paddock, local businessman and friend of the Wilders, asks Almanzo if he would like to go into business with him making wagons and carts, Almanzo has an important decision to make. It is no surprise when Almanzo decides to stay on the farm and help his father.

Vocabulary Lists

The vocabulary words which are listed below, correspond to each section of *Farmer Boy*, as outlined in the table of contents. The words with hyphens are how the words appear in *Farmer Boy*. They may no longer use hyphens. Vocabulary ideas and activities are found on the following page.

Section 1

trudged	impudently	boughs	billows	bobsled
tardiness	headcheese	thrash	fullcloth	muffler
blacksnake whip	dyed	schoolhouse	bureau	nightcap
primer	lye	tallow	bow-pin	nuzzle
hoopskirts	swaggered	gangling	placidly	manger

Section 2

new-fangled	fetched	caldron	eaves	harrowed
calico	underwaist	drawers	auger	nubbin
stout	tin-peddler	colanders	askew	lavishly
moosewood boughs	crimped	homespun	currycomb	sedately
store-boughten	hindquarters	yoke	whitewash	whittle

Section 3

lugged	haunches	parasols	jeered	prowling
stealthy	merciful	shear	fifes	muzzles
dappled-gray	horsehair	dislocated	bleating	sheepfold
fleece	trousers	soft-soap	solemn	cannon
carding machine	bridles	churning	aggravating	ewes

Section 4

scythes	grindstones	poultice	swathes	crevice
meadowlarks	dinner horn	egg-nog	dipper	beechnuts
cracklings	whetstones	windrows	hay-rack	oat-straw
reapers	wig-wams	butter-buyer	rutabagas	withered
corn-shocks	cobbler	cider mill	parsnips	hogsheads

Section 5

mournful	undisturbed	scour	cuds	mending
flail	husks	fanning-mill	gratitude	apprentice
cant-poles	pocketbook	whirled	skinflint	maul
shinnied	sixpence	measly	wheelwright	switch
horehound candy	quaked	laprobe	capstan	liveryman

8

Vocabulary Activity Ideas

You can help your students learn and retain the vocabulary in *Farmer Boy* by providing them with interesting vocabulary activities. Here are a few ideas to try.

- Divide your class into teams. The teams find the words in the context of the book and define them. Members record the words and their meanings in a vocabulary notebook.

- Have your students create a **Picture Dictionary** of the words. Whenever possible, include real samples, such as a small square of calico, for the word "calico." Design a cover, have it laminated, and bind the finished work. Display it in a prominent place in the room. Donate it to the library at the end of the year.

- Have a **Vocabulary Bee**. This is similar to a Spelling Bee. The students must spell the word and define it.

- Play **Vocabulary Mum Ball**. One student throws a ball to another student, saying one of the vocabulary words, before throwing. The student who catches the ball must define the word to stay in the game. If a student can't define the word or drops the ball, he or she is out of the game.

- Using old gameboards, play **Vocabulary Champ**. One student is the "Vocabulary Master." The Master has cards with the vocabulary words on one side and their meaning on the other. Each student must give the correct definition in order to roll the dice and move. The Champ is the first person to reach the end of the gameboard.

- Play **Vocabulary Charades**. Words are acted out and teammates guess the correct answer.

- Encourage your students to **use the words** in their own writing each day. Have them dazzle their friends and family by using the words in their spoken language as well.

- Group your students into teams. Give each student a slate, a piece of chalk and a dictionary. Give the whole class one of the **words to define**, using the dictionary. Team members may help one another. Each member must write the definition on their slate. If everyone on the team has the correct answer, the team earns a point. (The teacher keeps score on the blackboard.) The team with the most points at the end of a given period of time is the winning team. Also, the teacher might give the meaning and the team members give the word, or the team may be requested to give the word and the correct part of speech, or they may be asked to write the word in a sentence.

- Ask your students to create paragraphs which use the vocabulary words to present **History Lessons** that relate to the time period of historical events mentioned in the story.

Quiz Time!

1. Who is the author of *Farmer Boy*? _____

2. On the back of this paper, list three major events of this section.

3. Describe the Hardscrabble Boys. _____

_____

_____

4. Who is Mr. Corse? Tell what he did to the Hardscrabble Boys. _____

_____

_____

5. Why is Almanzo not allowed to touch the horses? _____

_____

6. Who are Star and Bright? _____

_____

_____

7. On the back of this paper, describe Father.

8. Name two things Almanzo receives for his birthday. _____

_____

_____

9. How do Almanzo and Royal cover the ice? Why?_____

_____

_____

_____

10. What almost happens to Almanzo when they are cutting the ice? _____

_____

_____

_____

Making Fried Apples 'n' Onions

They talked about spareribs, and turkey with dressing, and baked beans, and crackling cornbread, and other good things. But Almanzo said that what he liked most in the world was fried apples 'n' onions...Mother knew what he liked best, and she had cooked it for him.

Ingredients:

- ½ pound (230g) of sliced bacon
- 6 yellow onions
- 6 tart apples
- 2 tablespoons (30 mL) of brown sugar
- 1 tablespoon (15 mL) of cinnamon

Directions:

In a 12-inch (30 cm) skillet, fry bacon until brown and crisp. Set aside. Peel and slice onions. Core and slice apples, crosswise, in circles, about ¼ inch (.6 cm) thick. Drain all but about 1 tablespoon of fat from the skillet, add onion slices. Cook over medium heat for about three minutes. Cover with apple slices. Sprinkle with brown sugar and cinnamon. Cover and cook until tender. Serve with bacon. (Serves 6)

Find a recipe that uses either apples or onions, or both. Write the recipe in the space provided.

(recipe title)

Ingredients

_____   _____   _____

_____   _____   _____

Directions

_____

_____

_____

_____

_____

_____

_____

One-Room Schoolhouse

Materials

- chalk and a small slate for each child
- a teacher's bell
- small booklets for each child to write in (These may be teacher made.)
- a small bench or a row of chairs
- pioneer outfits for the teacher and the students (Overalls and suspenders for the boys, long dresses and bonnets for the girls.)

Directions:

Arrange your classroom so the boys' desks are all on one side of the room and the girls' desks are on the other side. Place your desk in the center, at the front of the room. When the teacher rings the bell the one-room schoolhouse will begin. When the bell is rung again, in about one hour, the one-room schoolhouse will end. Place the small bench (or row of chairs) in front of your desk. Give each child a slate, a small booklet, and a piece of chalk.

Tell the children they are not allowed to speak unless they are spoken to. Have students neatly copy a proverb onto the slate. (See some examples in the box below.) When they are finished, they must sit quietly on the bench and wait for the teacher to ask them to come to his or her desk with their slates. Only three children are allowed on the bench at a time. If the teacher approves of the work, the students may quietly return to their seats and copy the proverb neatly into their books and memorize it. When students have completed this task, they may quietly sit on the bench and wait for the teacher to ask them to recite the proverb. If their writing has been done well, they may copy the math problems from the board and continue the same way.

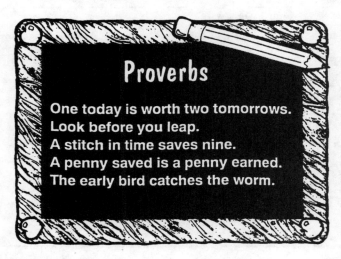

Proverbs

One today is worth two tomorrows.
Look before you leap.
A stitch in time saves nine.
A penny saved is a penny earned.
The early bird catches the worm.

When finished with this activity, the students gather in small groups and discuss their experience. Later, have a whole group discussion. Have students write about their experience and compare schools of yesterday and today. Ask them to tell which they prefer and why.

Popcorn Magic

Popcorn is American. Nobody but the Indians ever had popcorn, till after the Pilgrim Fathers came to America.... Almanzo looked at every kernel before he ate it...You can fill a glass full to the brim with milk and fill another glass of the same size brim full of popcorn, and then you can put all the popcorn kernel by kernel into the milk, and the milk will not run over. You cannot do this with bread. Popcorn and milk are the only two things that will go into the same place.

Is Almanzo right? Do the following experiment to find out.

I. Predict what will happen if you

    A. fill a glass with popped popcorn and another glass of the same size with milk, and place the popcorn, kernel by kernel, into the glass of milk.

    B. fill a glass with pieces of bread and another glass of the same size with milk, and place the bread, piece by piece, into the glass of milk.

II. Do the experiment above, and record your results.

III. Conclusion: Was Almanzo right?

Note to the teacher: It may be helpful to have the students work in teams. Record their predictions and the results of their experiments on the chart below and discuss. (Tomie dePaola's book, *The Popcorn Book,* Holiday House, 1978, is a good introduction to this lesson.)

	Prediction	Result
Popcorn		
Bread		

From Past to Present

Tell the students you are going to take a trip into their imaginations. Ask them to close their eyes and imagine as you read the following passage:

> *Almanzo lived, as a young boy, over one hundred years ago. Things are very different now. Imagine yourself at school today. Now imagine Almanzo at school back then. Think of the one-room schoolhouse, the Hardscrabble Boys, and Mr. Corse.*

Allow time for them to visualize before opening their eyes.

Ask the students to share what they saw with one another, and as a whole group. Discuss and compare similarities and differences.

Using the picture frame below, have your students illustrate Almanzo at school on one side. On the other side, have them illustrate themselves at school.

On the lines below the frame, and on the back of this page, have the students write a comparison of their experiences and Almanzo's.

Note to the Teacher: Their pages could be displayed on a bulletin board or compiled and bound into a book, entitled "From Past to Present."

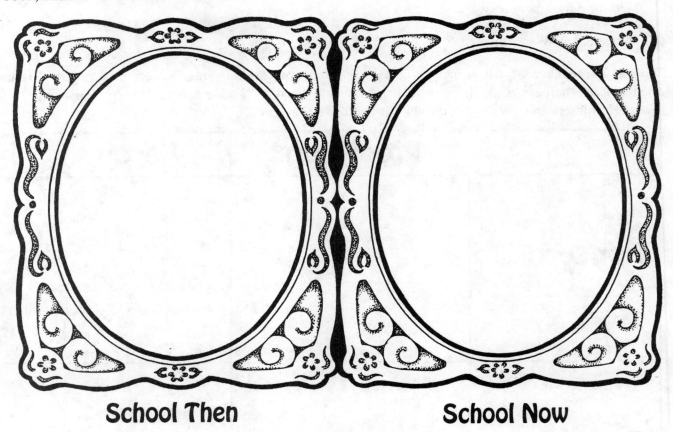

School Then   **School Now**

_____

_____

_____

Quiz Time!

1. How does Almanzo feel about taking a bath? _____

    _____

2. Describe how Almanzo takes his bath. _____

    _____

3. What does Father own that makes him proud because they are some of the best in New York State?

    _____

    _____

4. What does Frank have that Almanzo wants? _____

5. What does Almanzo make out of moosewood boughs? _____

    _____

    _____

6. On the back of this paper, list three things that happen in this section.

7. On a clean sheet of drawing paper, illustrate the tin peddler. Tell what Almanzo thought of him. If you were Almanzo, what would you like to buy from the tin peddler?

    _____

    _____

8. What does Almanzo do on Sunday? What do you do on Sunday? Tell how your day is different from Almanzo's. _____

    _____

9. What happens to Almanzo, Pierre, and Louis when they decide to take Star and Bright for a ride in the snow? _____

    _____

    _____

10. Describe how you felt when you read about the ride in the snow. _____

    _____

    _____

    _____

Make a Scene

In every maple tree Father had bored a small hole, and fitted a little wooden spout into it. Sweet maple sap was dripping from the spouts into small pails.

Today syrup is gathered from maple trees in much the same way. Small spouts are bored into maple trees in early spring. The syrup is then refined by boiling. It is later bottled for shipping. Create a diorama which shows Father and Almanzo making maple syrup, as depicted in chapter 10.

Materials:

- shoeboxes
- oaktag
- maple twigs
- paste
- tempera paint
- construction paper
- scissors
- clay

Directions:

Place a shoebox on its side, lengthwise. Using construction paper and paint, design the background scene on the inside walls of the shoebox. Using the twigs, create maple trees by inserting the bottom into a small mound of clay to allow the trees to be free standing. Cut figures for Almanzo and Father from the oaktag.

Note to Teacher:

If possible, visit a sugarbush with your class. If this isn't possible a unit on sugaring might be helpful. Fresh maple syrup or maple sugar might be an added treat for your class.

Display finished work in the classroom or library.

What a Character

Students will enjoy making oversize characters and props to display on a giant story mural in the classroom.

Materials:

- butcher paper, construction paper, scissors, glue, paints, crayons, markers, yarn, fabric scraps, crumpled newspaper, tissue, etc.

Directions:

1. Assign a small group of students a scene to illustrate.

2. Have students cut out giant objects (trees, rocks, animals, etc.) from butcher paper, and decorate with art materials.

3. Help students make giant story characters by having one student lie down on a large sheet of butcher paper while another students traces around the body.

4. Using the descriptions given in the book of Almanzo, Royal, Mother, Father, Alice, and Eliza Jane, have students cut out the body outlines and decorate them with art materials.

5. Help students cut out and glue, or staple patterns together around the edges, leaving an open end to stuff with crumpled newspaper or cotton balls. Have students glue or staple the open edge after stuffing.

6. Arrange props on the bulletin board, classroom wall, or in the library. Have students create word bubbles for each character.

7. Have the class read the story aloud. Invite another class in, and share your creation with them.

Research and Present

To gain a better appreciation of pioneer living, visit your school library or local museum. Using resources such as the encyclopedia, the card catalog, and the almanac, choose one of the topics below as a research project:

1. Tin peddlers of the past.

2. Oxen: how and why they were once used for farming.

3. Seasons: their affect on pioneer living.

4. Childhood in the late 1800's.

5. Games and toys of the late 1800's.

6. Training horses.

7. One-room schoolhouses.

8. Growing pumpkins.

Give an oral presentation to the class on your findings. You might dress in character for your presentations, as a tin peddler, historian, research scientist, or as a child of the 1800's. This will help to bring history to life in the classroom. Write your outline in the space below and use it while giving your presentation.

(topic)

Sit Perfectly Still!

Boys must not run or laugh or talk loudly on Sunday....

... Almanzo just sat. He had to. He was not allowed to do anything else, for Sunday was not a day for working or playing. It was a day for going to church and for sitting still.

Close your eyes and imagine what it would be like to sit perfectly still for an entire day. On the lines provided, write a journal entry about how you think you might feel.

_____

_____

_____

_____

_____

Sit perfectly still and quietly as Almanzo did. Try it for five or ten minutes. Pretend that it is Sunday all day, don't run, laugh, or talk loudly. On the lines below, write a journal entry about your pretend Sunday experience. Tell how it made you feel.

_____

_____

_____

_____

_____

_____

_____

_____

_____

Quiz Time!

1. Father and his helpers claim that they will finish shearing the sheep before Almanzo. How does Almanzo trick them?

   _____

2. Father said, "He laughs best who laughs last." What does he mean? _____

   _____

3. On the back of this paper, describe Almanzo's cousin, Frank.

4. What happens when Frank dares Almanzo to ask Father for a nickel?_____

   _____

5. What happens when Almanzo throws the blacking brush at Eliza Jane? _____

   _____

6. How does Almanzo feel when the Webbs come for a visit and they all go into the parlor?

   _____

   _____

7. Lucy the Pig eats the candy that Almanzo and Alice made. Describe what happened.

   _____

   _____

8. Name three ways in which Almanzo's celebration of Independence Day differs from your own.

   _____

   _____

   _____

9. How does the strange dog protect Almanzo and his family? _____

   _____

   _____

   _____

10. When Almanzo is picking berries by himself, he meets an animal in the forest. What is it?

   _____

Mother Wilder's Blueberry Pudding

Ingredients: *(Serves six)*

- 10 ounces (280 g) of blueberries
- 4 tablespoons (60 mL) of butter
- 1 egg
- ¾ cup (180 mL) homogenized milk
- ½ teaspoons (3 mL) baking soda
- 1 ½ cups (350 mL) white flour
- 1 cup (250 mL) sugar
- 1 teaspoon (5 mL) cream of tartar
- 1 ½ quart (about 1 L) pudding mold with a lid (or a clean 2 pound/1 kg coffee can)

Directions:

- Wash and drain berries. Generously grease inside the mold and its lid with soft butter.
- Beat egg, stir in milk and baking soda. In another bowl, mix flour, sugar and cream of tartar. Work in remaining butter until mixture is uniformly coarse. Stir liquid into dry mixture until all is moist. Stir in blueberries last.
- Pour batter into mold and cover tightly. Set the container in a large kettle and fill the kettle two-thirds full with boiling water.
- Cover and simmer for 1 ½ hours or longer. Unmold the finished pudding onto a platter. Enjoy!
- Make a class recipe book using the cover below. You may wish to include this recipe and the fried apples 'n' onions recipe from page 11.

Classy Recipes

by

Readers' Theater

Readers' Theater is a style of performance done before an audience by players who may be dressed as characters from a book. The players work in teams selecting a passage from the book to reenact. They write a script, practice performing, choose costumes, and recreate the scene for their audience.

Materials: one large trunk filled with a collection of costumes; one popcorn popper and popcorn; tickets

Bring the characters from *Farmer Boy* into your classroom. In teams of four or five, choose a scene from the book (a quick way to get started with this technique is to duplicate the desired passages directly from the book, and have the students highlight their parts). Choose costumes from the theater trunk and practice, practice, practice!

When your team is ready to present, give each member of the audience a ticket to the performance. Have a "ticket taker" stand by the classroom door and collect the tickets as the audience enters. Assign someone the task of popcorn maker. Have him or her make popcorn and pass it out before the performance.

Possible Scenes:

Almanzo throws the blacking brush at Eliza Jane

Lucy the Pig eats the candy

Mr. Corse whips Big Bill Ritchie

Almanzo finds Mr. Thompson's wallet

Mr. Paddock offers Almanzo a job

Tips for acting:

Speak loudly and clearly.

Practice your lines so you can say them without a script.

Use expression and emotion; pretend you really are that character.

Have fun!

Pumpkins Anyone?

Father taught Almanzo how to raise a milk-fed pumpkin.

Following the directions below, plant your own pumpkins and chart their growth. You can add to this lesson by baking pumpkin seeds, carving a class pumpkin, or making pumpkin cookies.

Materials:

- potting soil (two bags)
- small milk cartons (one per student)
- pumpkin seeds

Directions:

Rinse the milk carton and fill with potting soil. Plant your pumpkin seed and cover with topsoil. Water lightly. Place near a window. Water lightly every other day. Using a ruler, measure its growth each week. Keep a record of its growth with the chart below.

Pumpkin Growth Chart	
Name:	
Date:	**Growth in Inches**

Independence Day

Compare your Independence Day celebration with Almanzo's. On the firecrackers below, tell how they are alike and how they are different.

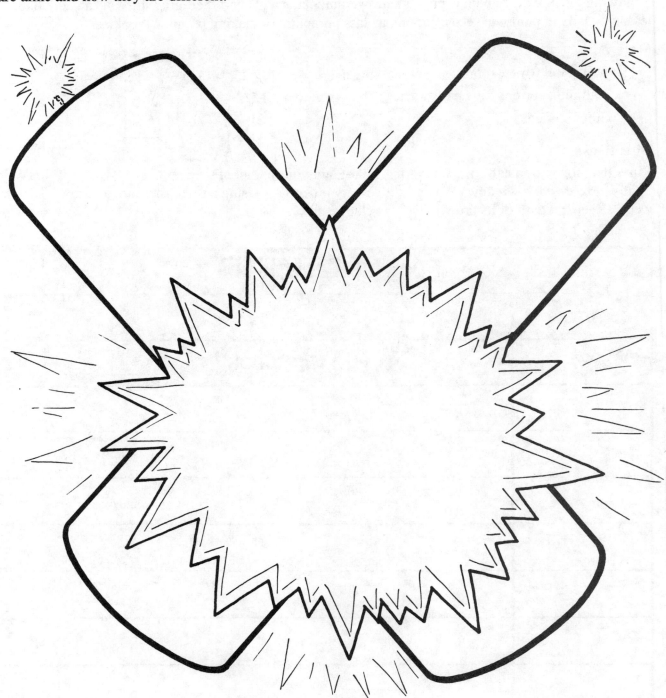

Pretend you are a newspaper reporter. Write an article which advertises an Independence Day celebration of today. Design a poster for it. Share your article and poster in small groups and discuss. Have a whole class discussion on the differences between today's celebration and Almanzo's.

Quiz Time!

1. On the back of this paper, describe what happens when the butter-buyer comes to Almanzo's house.

2. What happens when Almanzo's scalding hot potato bursts?_____

_____

3. Do you think Father should have sent Almanzo home after he was injured? Tell why. _____

_____

_____

_____

4. On the back of this paper, describe the County Fair.

5. What does Almanzo win for his milk-fed pumpkin at the fair? _____

_____

6. On the back of this paper, write a descriptive paragraph of the cobbler.

7. In the chapter, "Fall of the Year," Almanzo has many jobs to do. List three of them.

_____

_____

_____

8. Where do Royal, Alice, and Eliza Jane go to school?_____

_____

_____

9. How does Almanzo feel with Alice, Royal, and Eliza Jane gone? _____

_____

_____

10. Describe Almanzo's bobsled. _____

_____

_____

_____

Candlemaking

All one day Almanzo helped Mother make candles. That night, they had made enough candles to last till butchering-time next year.

Material:
- paraffin (old crayons or candles may also be used)
- 2 coffee cans
- small hot plate
- cotton string
- pot larger than coffee cans
- water
- potholders or oven mitts
- dowels or long pencils

Preparation:
1. Heat the water on the stove in a large pot. The water level should be lower than the top of a coffee can.

2. Put a paraffin slab into an empty coffee can. Carefully, place the can into a pot of hot water. Allow the wax to melt.

3. Prepare the wick by cutting a length of string twice the depth of the can (about 12"/30 cm for a double candle and 6"/15 cm for a single candle).

4. Fill a second coffee can with ice water.

Directions:

Place the wick over the wooden dowel. Dip it first into the hot wax, and then into cold water. Go back and forth until your candle grows to the size you like. If making a single candle, tie the string to the dowel or pencil before dipping.

Hang the dipped candles from a coat hanger to dry. Clothespins may be used to hold the candles in place. Cut double candles apart.

Caution:

Never allow children to work unsupervised.

Paraffin is dangerous. Never boil, overheat, or mix with water. It should only be melted over heated water. Wax can ignite and smoke terribly.

Never melt the wax directly over a heat source. Use a double boiler or a can within a can of water. Warm wax makes a better candle than hot wax. Wax fires must be smothered. Treat hot wax just as you would hot oil.

Create a Model of Almanzo's Farm

Almanzo's farm stood quietly proud on the peaceful landscape. With a friend, choose a building from the list below in creating a model for your classroom of Almanzo's homestead.

Materials:

- construction paper
- small boxes
- tissue paper
- 3'x 4' (1 m x 1.2 m) heavy cardboard or plywood
- tempera paint
- scraps of fabric
- small plastic animals (optional)
- wallpaper scraps

In teams of two or three, recreate one building from the following list. The numbers in parentheses refer to the page number in the book, *Farmer Boy*.

- Almanzo's House (pages 13-14)
- The Horse Barn (page 14)
- The Big Barn (pages 14-15)
- The South Barn (page 15)
- The Board Fence (page 15)
- The Schoolhouse (pages 4-13)

Directions:

Using one of the boxes, paint the outside, and design the inside (e.g. place scraps of fabric on the windows for curtains, wallpaper the walls, create furniture, etc.). Cover the heavy cardboard or plywood with green construction paper or paint for grass, and mount the finished products on top. Horses, cows, oxen, and even Lucy the pig may be added for a finished touch!

Poetry Anyone?

There are many forms of poetry. Poetry that contains both rhyme and rhythm is often popular with students. All rhyming poems contain a rhyme scheme. A rhyme scheme tells the rhyming pattern of a poem. The poem below contains an ABCB rhyme scheme because the second and fourth lines rhyme and the first and third do not.

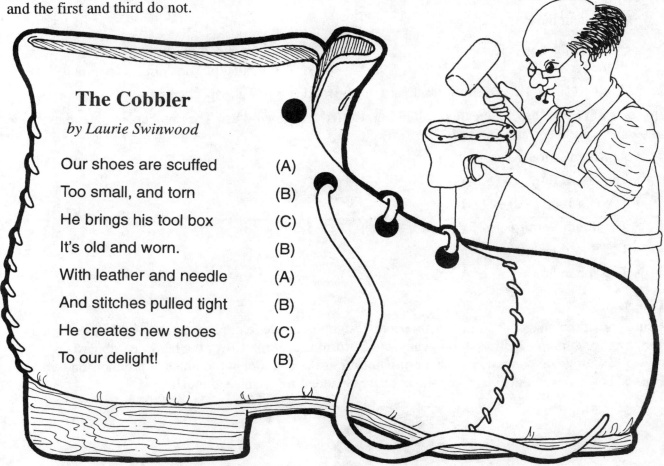

The Cobbler
by Laurie Swinwood

Our shoes are scuffed	(A)
Too small, and torn	(B)
He brings his tool box	(C)
It's old and worn.	(B)
With leather and needle	(A)
And stitches pulled tight	(B)
He creates new shoes	(C)
To our delight!	(B)

Using the ABCB rhyme scheme, have students write poems about the cobbler. Have them illustrate the poems.

Compile students poetry and illustrations into a book. Have a team design the cover, laminate it, and bind the book with a binding machine or with a zigzag stitch on a sewing machine. Display in the classroom. Place a library pocket and card in the back, and allow the children to sign it out to take home and share with family and friends.

There's No Place Like Home

The roof of the tall red-painted house was rounded with snow, and from all the eaves hung a fringe of great icicles...candlelight shone in all the windows.

Almanzo's home was the center of his life. In the frame below illustrate your home. On the lines below write a descriptive paragraph about your home. Be sure to include your favorite rooms, fragrances, foods, and family activities.

Quiz Time!

1. On the back of this page, describe Almanzo's Christmas.

2. Compare your Christmas to Almanzo's. Which would you prefer? Why?_____

    _____

    _____

3. On the back of this paper, write a descriptive paragraph of Mr. Thompson.

4. Why does Almanzo give the nickel back to Mr. Thompson? _____

    _____

5. What is a "boughten cap"? _____

    _____

6. Describe how the boys played snowfort._____

    _____

    _____

7. Why doesn't Almanzo have to go to school in January? _____

    _____

8. Tell what happens to Almanzo when the log falls on him. _____

    _____

    _____

9. What does Mr. Paddock want Almanzo to do? _____

    _____

    _____

10. What does Almanzo decide to be when he grows up? What do you think of his decision?

    _____

    _____

    _____

    _____

Farmer Boy Doll

Materials:

- patterns (pages 32-33)
- two 9" x 12" squares of white felt
- colored scraps of fabric (for clothing)
- markers
- two black buttons (for eyes)
- black yarn (for hair)

- 1 ounce (30 g) fiberfill
- craft glue or hot glue gun
- red craft pencil
- black thread and needle
- pencil

Directions:

1. Place one piece of felt on top of the other. Pin the pattern pieces for the body and the hat in the center.

2. Cut around the edges of the doll and hat patterns.

3. With black thread and a needle, attach the black button eyes as indicated on the pattern piece. Using a red craft pencil, draw a mouth.

4. Using white craft glue or a hot glue gun, seal along the outer edges of the body. Leave the marked area open.

5. Stuff lightly with fiberfill through opening. The eraser end of a pencil is useful for stuffing the arms and legs. Glue opening closed.

6. Cut 25 strips of yarn (each 2"/ 5 cm long), and glue in place around head. Trim to desired length.

7. Fold fabric scraps in half, with right sides together. Place clothing pattern pieces in middle and pin in place. Cut around the outer edges of pattern. Place wrong sides together and glue with a fine line of glue along the inside edges as the dotted line on the pattern indicates. Be sure to leave openings free.

8. After gluing shirt pieces together cut up the front of the shirt indicated by the dashed lines on the shirt pattern. After putting the shirt on the doll, glue shut.

9. After gluing pant pieces together cut a fly in the front of the pants as indicated by the dashed line on the pants pattern. After putting the pants on the doll, glue the fly shut.

10. Dress the doll in the shirt and pants. Attach the suspenders in the front by gluing them under the pants edge, then crossing them in the back and gluing them in the same manner.

11. Use markers and extra buttons to decorate the dolls' clothing if desired. If you do not wish to make the clothes, you may draw them onto the felt doll with markers.

12. Glue hat pieces as indicated on the pattern. Decorate if you wish. Place hat on his head and glue down to hold securely.

Patterns

Patterns *(cont.)*

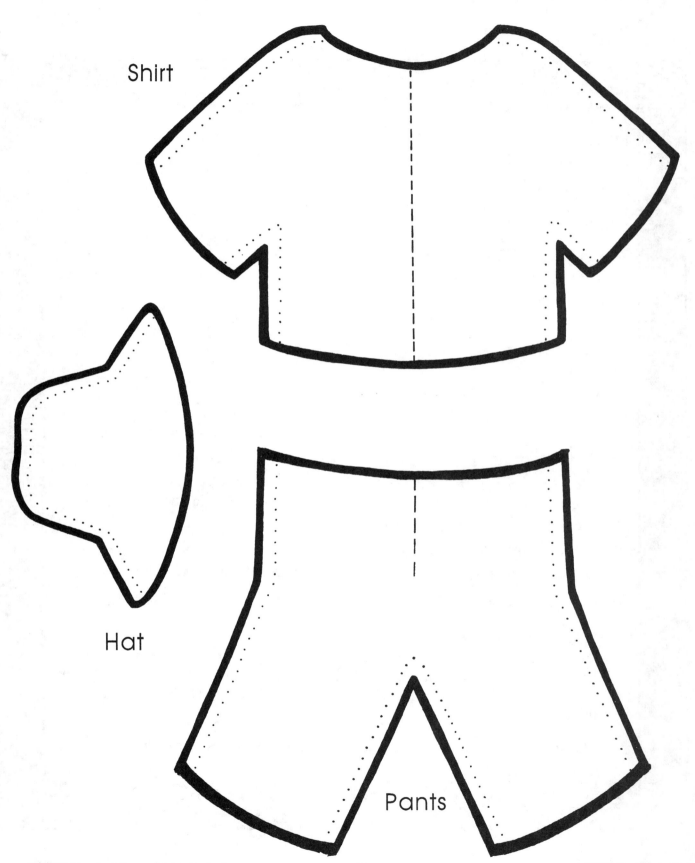

Shirt

Hat

Pants

Farmer Boy Quilt

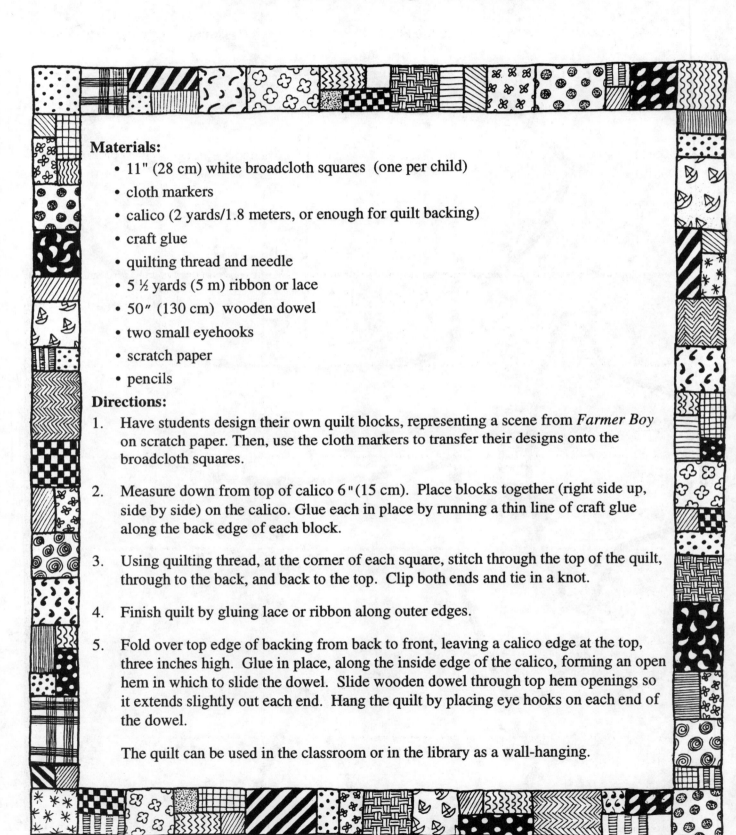

Materials:

- 11" (28 cm) white broadcloth squares (one per child)
- cloth markers
- calico (2 yards/1.8 meters, or enough for quilt backing)
- craft glue
- quilting thread and needle
- 5 ½ yards (5 m) ribbon or lace
- 50" (130 cm) wooden dowel
- two small eyehooks
- scratch paper
- pencils

Directions:

1. Have students design their own quilt blocks, representing a scene from *Farmer Boy* on scratch paper. Then, use the cloth markers to transfer their designs onto the broadcloth squares.

2. Measure down from top of calico 6" (15 cm). Place blocks together (right side up, side by side) on the calico. Glue each in place by running a thin line of craft glue along the back edge of each block.

3. Using quilting thread, at the corner of each square, stitch through the top of the quilt, through to the back, and back to the top. Clip both ends and tie in a knot.

4. Finish quilt by gluing lace or ribbon along outer edges.

5. Fold over top edge of backing from back to front, leaving a calico edge at the top, three inches high. Glue in place, along the inside edge of the calico, forming an open hem in which to slide the dowel. Slide wooden dowel through top hem openings so it extends slightly out each end. Hang the quilt by placing eye hooks on each end of the dowel.

The quilt can be used in the classroom or in the library as a wall-hanging.

Take a Field Trip!

Travel to a modern day farm, or take an imaginary trip to a modern farm through books and slides in the library. Take notes!

If it isn't possible to bring your students to a modern day farm, then bring the farm to them! Borrow slides, books, pictures, etc. from your library. If possible, invite a local farmer to your classroom. Have him or her do a presentation on modern farming.

Hold a class discussion on students' charts. Discuss the differences and similarities between farming in Almanzo's day and today.

Directions:

Compare Almanzo's farm to farms of today, using the chart below.

	Almanzo's Farm	Modern Farms
Tools Used		
Crops Planted		
Machinery		
Animals		
Farm Buildings		

Decisions, Decisions!

Almanzo squirmed. Father was looking at him too hard, and so was Mother...He wanted to be just like Father. But he didn't want to say so.

Almanzo is asked to make some very important decisions at a young age. He decides to become a farmer like his father. Visit your local chapter of 4-H and inquire about farming today. On the chart below, list reasons why you would become a farmer and reasons why you wouldn't. If you were Almanzo, what would your final decision be? Circle your answer below.

Reasons for Being a Farmer	Reasons for Not Being a Farmer

If I were Almanzo I (would, would not) become a farmer.

Note to Teacher:

Have the students share their charts. Discuss the results. Set up a debate between two teams. On one side put those who would become farmers; on the other side, those who wouldn't. Discuss their reasons for each.

Any Questions?

When you finished reading *Farmer Boy*, did you have some questions that were left unanswered? Write some of your questions here.

_____

_____

_____

Work in groups or by yourself to prepare possible answers for some or all of the questions you have asked above and those written below. When you finish your predictions, share your ideas with the class.

- Where did Mr. Corse sleep when he stayed at Almanzo's house?

- Jonas Lane, the teacher from the year before, died because he was beaten so badly by the Hardscrabble Boys. Why weren't the boys punished for his death?

- Does Big Bill Ritchie ever come back to school?

- Whatever happened to Mr. Corse, the schoolteacher?

- Why does Almanzo get to stay home from school on his birthday?

- Why doesn't Father spank Almanzo when he almost falls into the water when they are cutting ice?

- The potato burned Almanzo's eye. Why doesn't Father take him home?

- Would the robbers have broken into the Wilders' home and stolen the money for the colts if the strange dog hadn't scared them away?

- What does Father mean when he says, "He laughs best who laughs last?"

- Why does Father give Almanzo a half dollar when he only asks for a nickel?

- Why doesn't Eliza Jane tell her parents about Almanzo throwing the blacking brush?

- Does Mother ever find out about the patched wallpaper in the parlor?

- How does finding Mr. Thompson's pocketbook affect Almanzo's life?

- How would Almanzo's life have been different if he'd decided to be an apprentice to Mr. Paddock?

- Is Almanzo happy as a farmer?

Book Report Ideas

There are many ways to do a book report. After you have finished reading *Farmer Boy*, choose one method of reporting that interests you. It may be a way your teacher suggests, an idea of your own, or one of the ways below.

- **From the Artist**

  A model of a scene from the story can be created, or a likeness of one or more of the characters from the story can be drawn or sculpted.

- **Time Capsule**

  Make a time capsule for future readers. Neatly print your reasons why *Farmer Boy* is such a good book. Store your time capsule in the library for future readers.

- **Come to Life!**

  As a group, dress as characters from a scene in the book. Using props act out that scene for the rest of the class.

- **Into the Future**

  This report predicts what might happen if *Farmer Boy* were to continue. It may take the form of a story in narrative or dramatic form or a visual display.

- **Twenty Questions**

  A reporter gives a series of clues about a character or an event in the story, in a vague to precise, general to specific order. After all clues have been given, the identity of the mystery character or event is guessed.

- **A Character Comes to Life!**

  Suppose one of the characters in *Farmer Boy* came to life and walked into your home or school. Write about what the character sees, hears, and feels as he or she experiences the world in which you live.

- **Sales Talk**

  Dress as a salesperson. Write a sales pitch and design some kind of graphics in an effort to sell *Farmer Boy* to your classmates.

- **Coming Attraction!**

  Farmer Boy is about to be made into a movie, and you have been chosen to design the promotional poster. Include the title and author of the book, a listing of the main characters and the contemporary actors who will play them, illustrate a scene from the book, and write a brief synopsis of the story.

- **Literary Interview**

  This report is done in pairs. One student will pretend to be a character in the story, and will be dressed as that character. The other student will play the role of a television or radio interviewer trying to provide the audience with insights into the character's life and personality.

Research Ideas

Describe three things that you read in *Farmer Boy* that you would like to learn more about.

1. _____

2. _____

3. _____

As you read *Farmer Boy*, you encountered true-life people and events, pioneer customs and celebrations, ways of speaking, delicious foods, and the lifestyle of pioneer farmers. To increase your understanding of the characters and events of the book, as well as to appreciate Laura Ingalls Wilder's craft as a writer, research to find out more about these people, places, and things.

Work in groups to research one or more of the areas you named above or the areas that are listed below. Share your findings with the rest of the class in any appropriate format for oral presentation.

- Malone, N.Y.
- sheep shearing
- maple syrup
- sugaring
- cutting ice
- oxen
- weaving
- spinning
- pioneer

    education

    home life

    families

    clothing

    medical practices

    cooking

    farming

    celebrations

- one-room schoolhouse
- making candy
- cobblers
- apprenticeship
- Fourth of July celebrations
- popcorn:

    its origin

    different types

    growing seasons

- Recipes
- The Wilders:

    What became of each
        one after *Farmer Boy*?

    When and where did
        Almanzo meet Laura Ingalls?

Have a Read-A-Thon

See how many of Laura Ingalls Wilder's books, listed below, you can read. Color in the covered wagon beside each book as you complete it.

Ideas for Reading:

- Read aloud to a younger brother or sister.
- Ask your parents to take turns reading to you at night.
- Read into a tape recorder and share the recording with a friend.
- Read with a friend.
- Invite younger children in to hear some stories being read. Wear a costume representative of the time.
- Do a read-around in small groups reading the same books.

Little House in the Big Woods
This is Laura's first book. It tells about her early life in the Big Woods of Wisconsin.

Little House on the Prairie
Pa sold their snug log cabin in Wisconsin and bought a covered wagon. They moved to Indian country in Oklahoma.

Farmer Boy
Laura wrote this book to tell about her husband's early pioneer childhood. He and his family lived on a large farm in northern New York.

On the Banks of Plum Creek
Laura and her family live in a dugout on Plum Creek, in Minnesota. They meet Nellie Oleson, a snobbish town girl. Laura is full of mischief, and one of her best pranks involves Nellie.

The Long Winter
The Ingalls barely survive a long cold winter in De Smet, South Dakota. The snow is so deep that the entire first floor of their house is buried.

Little Town on the Prairie
The long hard winter is finally over in De Smet. Laura works many hours to earn money to help send Mary to the college for the blind.

These Happy Golden Years
Laura shares her experiences as a young schoolteacher. Here she meets and marries young Almanzo Wilder.

40

Host a Wilder Celebration

Invite family, and friends to a Wilder Celebration in your classroom. Create invitations. Roll them up like scrolls, tie them with ribbon, and deliver them in person to family and friends.

Ideas for your Celebration:

• Dress as pioneer children and decorate the room with your life-sized characters of the Wilders.

• Display your Farmer Boy dolls and quilt, your illustrations, written work, and candles.

• Have Fried Apples 'n' Onions simmering in the Taster's Corner.

• Put on a Readers' Theater skit for your guests.

• Read the poems you have written.

• The authentic home of "Farmer Boy" has been purchased by The Almanzo and Laura Ingalls Wilder Association. Their dream is to restore the homestead, so fans may see it as it was when Almanzo and his family lived there. Each year thousands of fans, from all over the world, visit Almanzo's home. Perhaps your class could help in this worthwhile project by sharing this information with your guests and collecting pennies for the farm. For more information write to:

> ***The Almanzo and Laura Ingalls Wilder Association***
> P.O. Box 283
> Malone, New York 12953

• Put up a bulletin board that shows the differences in farming during Almanzo's time and now. Cover a bulletin board with green paper. Using a border made out of anything that might be produced on a farm such as cotton or dried corn husks, divide the board into two sections. Title the whole board "Farming." Title one side "How Almanzo Farmed" and the other side "How We Farm Today."

Enlarge the pattern on page 42 using a copy machine or an opaque projector. Color them. Place them on the side titled "How Almanzo Farmed." For the "How We Farm Today" section have students create a collage using magazines, their own drawings, or reproductions from books. Student textbooks are a good resource.

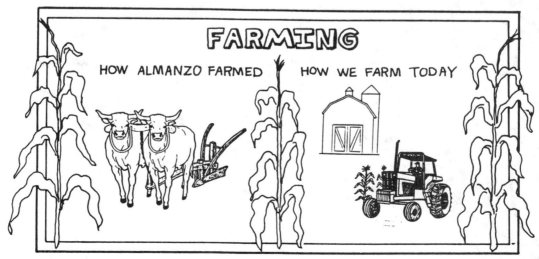

Bulletin Board Patterns

Objective Test and Essay

Matching:

Match the descriptions of the characters with their names.

1. _____ Almanzo   A. bossy older sister

2. _____ Mother   B. businessman who offers an apprenticeship

3. _____ Father   C. hardworking man, who takes pride in his farm

4. _____ Alice   D. Almanzo's favorite sister

5. _____ Eliza Jane   E. hardworking, gentle woman and a wonderful cook

6. _____ Royal   F. firm but loving older brother

7. _____ Cousin Frank   G. young boy who loves to brag and tease Almanzo

8. _____ Mr. Thompson   H. schoolteacher who handled Hardscrabble Boys

9. _____ Mr. Corse   I. miserly, selfish old man

10. _____ Mr. Paddock   J. a future farmer

True or False: Answer true or false in the blank below.

1. _____ Almanzo decides to become an apprentice to Mr. Paddock.

2. _____ Mr. Thompson is a kind and generous man.

3. _____ The Hardscrabble Boys were Almanzo's best friends.

4. _____ Eliza Jane mended the wallpaper in the parlor.

5. _____ Lucy the Pig's mouth was sealed shut with candy.

Essay: On the back of this paper, describe at least three ways that your life is different from Almanzo's. Who's life would you rather have?

Response

Explain the meaning of each of these quotations from *Farmer Boy*.

Chapter 1:   *They boasted that no teacher could finish the winter term in that school, and no teacher ever had.*

Chapter 4:   *Mr. Corse stepped away from his desk. His hand came from behind the desk lid, and a long, thin, black streak hissed through the air.*

Chapter 5:   *Almanzo did not go to school that day. He did not have to go to school when there were more important things to do.*

Chapter 6:   *He felt himself falling headlong into the dark water. His hands couldn't catch hold of anything. He knew he would sink and be drawn under the solid ice.*

Chapter 13:   *Mother stood listening and looking. It was dark under the trees, and she could not see anyone. But the dog growled savagely at the darkness.*

Chapter 14:   *No, you haven't beat me. I've got a fleece upstairs that you haven't sheared yet.*

Chapter 18:   *A great splash and smear of blacking appeared on the white-and-gold wallpaper.*

Chapter 21:   *Mr. Paddock said, 'I never saw a pumpkin beat it for size. How'd you raise such a big pumpkin, Almanzo?'*

Chapter 28:   *'Here,' he said, handing the nickel back. 'Keep your nickel. I can't change it.'*

Chapter 29:   *'I want a colt,' Almanzo said. 'Could I buy a colt all my own with some of that two hundred dollars, and would you let me break him?'*

Teacher Note:

Choose an appropriate number of quotations for your students.

Conversations

Work in groups to write and perform the conversations that might have occurred in each of the following situations.

- Father and Mr. Corse create a plan as to how to handle the Hardscrabble Boys. *(2 people)*

- Big Bill Ritchie explaining to his father about Mr. Corse and his blacksnake whip. *(2 people)*

- Almanzo and Royal doing the spring cleaning. *(2 people)*

- Mother, Father, Almanzo, and Royal the morning after the strange dog scared away the robbers and their money was still safely in the house. *(4 people)*

- Almanzo's cousin, Frank, dares him to ask Father for a nickel. Father gives Almanzo a half dollar. Frank, his friends, and Almanzo's discussion when Almanzo tells them what Father gave him. *(4 people)*

- Almanzo tells his family about seeing a bear in the woods. His family responds to this. *(5 people)*

- Eliza Jane and Royal are left in charge of the house for a week, while Mother and Father visit family. There are chores to be done, but Alice and Almanzo would rather have fun. *(4 people)*

- The entire family spends three days at the County Fair. They are all tired but proud of their success on their way home from the fair. *(6 people)*

- Royal, James, Almanzo, and Frank choose sides for a huge snowball fight. Mother is appalled at how wet they are when they come inside. *(5 people)*

- Almanzo finds Mr. Thompson's pocketbook, with fifteen hundred dollars in it. When he returns it to him, Mr. Thompson calls Almanzo a "durn boy," and gives him a nickel. Mr. Paddock is very angry, and so is Almanzo! *(3 people)*

Bibliography of Related Reading

Books for Students

Giff, Patricia Reilly. *Laura Ingalls Wilder: Growing Up in the Little House*. (Puffin Books, 1987).

"Laura Ingalls: Growing Up on the Prairie." *Cobblestone.* (February, 1986).

Walker, Barbara M. *The Little House Diary.* (Madison Press, 1979)

Wilder, Laura Ingalls. *Little House in the Big Woods.* (Harper & Row, 1932)

　　Little House on the Prairie. (Harper & Row, 1935)

　　On the Banks of Plum Creek. (Harper & Row, 1937)

References and Teacher Resources

Anderson, W.T. *The Story of the Wilders.* (Museum and Home, 1973)

　　A Wilder in the West. (LIW Memorial Society, 1971)

　　"How the Little House Books Found a Publishing Home." *Language Arts.* (April, 1981)

　　A Biography, Laura Ingalls Wilder. (Harper & Collins, 1991)

Cooper, B. "Appeal of the Little House Books to Children." *Elementary English*. (October, 1965)

dePaola, Tomie. *The Popcorn Book*. (Holiday House, 1978)

McGann, A.M. "Laura Ingalls Wilder Month." *Instructor* (February, 1982)

Smith, Dorothy. *The Wilder Family Story*. (Almanzo and Laura Ingalls Wilder Assoc., 1991)

Cookbooks and Activities

Anderson, W.T. *The Horn Book's Laura Ingalls Wilder.* (The Horn Book Incl., 1987)

Carson, Eugenia. *The Laura Ingalls Wilder Songbook.* (Harper, 1968)

"Laura's Gingerbread." *Horn Book*. (December, 1953)

Walker, Barbara. *The Little House Cookbook*. (Harper & Row, 1979)

Answer Key

Page 10
1. Laura Ingalls Wilder is the author.
2. Accept appropriate answers.
3. Accept appropriate answers.
4. Mr. Corse is their teacher. He whipped the Hardscrabble Boys with Father's blacksnake whip.
5. Father feels that Almanzo is too young.
6. Star and Bright are Almanzo's oxen.
7. Accept appropriate answers.
8. Almanzo receives a new sled and a calf-yoke.
9. Almanzo and Royal cover the ice with sawdust to keep it from melting.
10. Almanzo almost falls through a hole in the ice.

Page 15
1. Almanzo hates taking baths.
2. Almanzo and his family take turns filling a tub in the kitchen for one another for their Saturday night baths.
3. Father owns Morgan horses.
4. Frank has a "boughten cap."
5. Almanzo makes a whip out of moosewood boughs.
6. Accept appropriate answers.
7. Accept appropriate answers.
8. Almanzo spends time at church on Sunday. The rest of the day he must remain quiet.
9. Almanzo, Pierre, and Louis are thrown into the snow.
10. Accept appropriate answers.

Page 20
1. Almanzo hides a sheep in the loft.
2. Father means that Almanzo had fooled them. He has a laugh on them.
3. Accept appropriate answers.
4. Father gives Almanzo a half dollar.
5. The brush hits the parlor wall and left a big black smudge on it. Almanzo runs and hides in the barn. He is afraid for when Father and Mother return and see the black smudge.
6. Almanzo is terrified when the Webbs come for a visit. He also feels ashamed because Mother is so proud of the parlor and he has ruined her beautiful wallpaper. He does not want to go into the parlor because he knows the black smudge is there.
7. Lucy's mouth was sealed closed. She ran away from Almanzo. They chased her, and caught her, and finally freed her mouth of the candy. Lucy squealed all of the squeals that she had held in all night!
8. Accept appropriate answers.
9. The strange dog scares away the robbers.
10. Almanzo meets a black bear in the woods.

Answer Key *(cont.)*

Page 25
1. Accept appropriate answers.
2. The potato hits Almanzo in the eye. It burns his eyelid and cheek. Father ties his handkerchief over it.
3. Accept appropriate answers.
4. Accept appropriate answers.
5. Almanzo won a blue ribbon for his milk-fed pumpkin at the fair.
6. Accept appropriate answers.
7. Almanzo has to help collect beechnuts, prepare the barns for winter, help with the butchering, and make candles.
8. Royal, Alice, and Eliza Jane go to school at the Academy in Malone.
9. Almanzo feels lonely. He even misses Eliza Jane!
10. Accept appropriate answers.

Page 30
1. Accept appropriate answers.
2. Accept appropriate answers.
3. Accept appropriate answers.
4. Almanzo gives the nickel back to Mr. Thompson because he is insulted by Mr. Thompson's rude and stingy manner.
5. A boughten cap is a hat that is not home made, but, rather, purchased at a store.
6. Accept appropriate responses.
7. Almanzo doesn't have to go to school in January because he is helping Father haul wood.
8. The log falls on top of Almanzo and he can't get up. Father and John lift it off of him, and Almanzo is okay.
9. Mr. Paddock wants Almanzo to become an apprentice to him, to learn to become a wheelwright.
10. Almanzo decides to become a farmer, like Father.

Page 43
1. J 2. E 3. C 4. D 5. A 6. F 7. G 8. I 9. H 10. B

1. F 2. F 3. F 4. T 5. T

Essay: Accept appropriate responses.

Page 44
Accept all reasonable and well supported responses and explanations.

Page 45
Perform the conversations in class. Ask students to respond to the conversations in several different ways, such as, "Are the conversations realistic?" or, "Are the words the characters say in keeping with their personalities?"